What Can You See?

Kate McGough

Can you see the trees?

 What can you see now?

Can you see the big cat in the tree?

 What can you see now?

Can you see the lizards in the tree?

 What can you see now?

Can you see the birds in the tree?

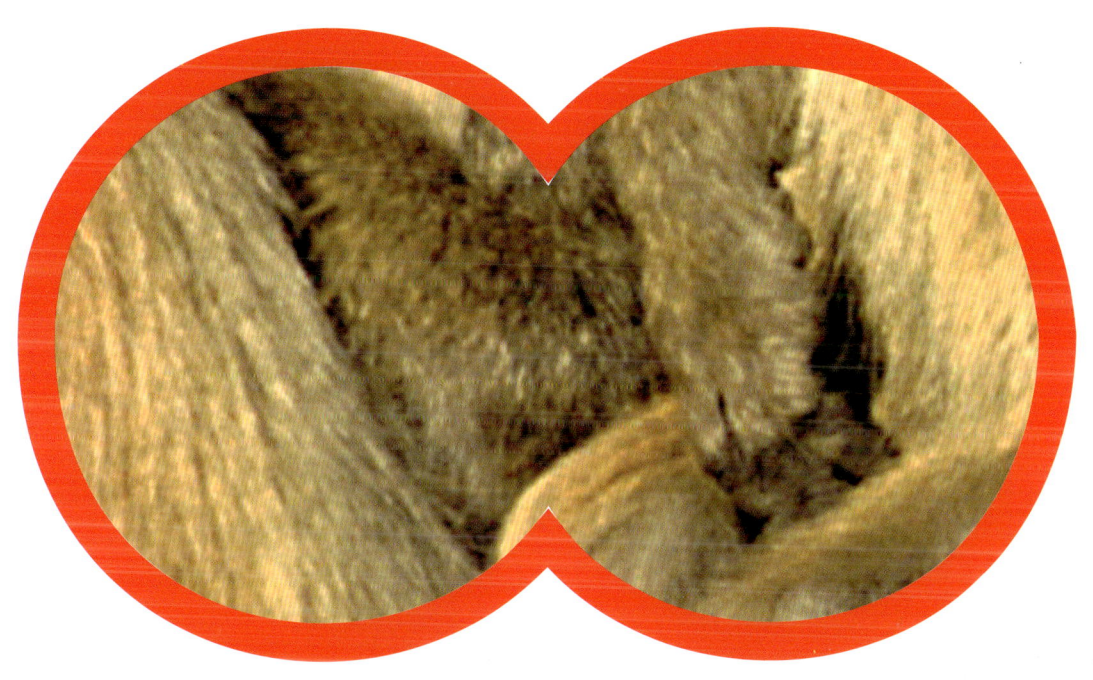

 What can you see now?

Can you see the monkeys in the tree?

1 big cat

2 lizards

3 birds

4 monkeys

Picture Index

 big cat 3–4

 birds 7–8

 lizards 5–6

 monkeys 9–10